OMEGA-ALPHA

OMEGA-ALPHA

TOBIAS TAOH

OMEGA-ALPHA

iUniverse books may be ordered through booksellers or by contacting:

iUniverse
1663 Liberty Drive
Bloomington, IN 47403
www.iuniverse.com
1-800-Authors (1-800-288-4677)

ISBN: 978-1-5320-6912-3 (sc)
ISBN: 978-1-5320-6913-0 (e)

Print information available on the last page.

iUniverse rev. date: 03/08/2019

OUT OF ASHES

OUT OF THE ASHES I CRY TO YOU LORD
IN MY DISTRESS THUS DO I FALTER
FOR THEY LAY TRAPS FOR MY SOUL
THEY ASSAULT BONES OF MY BODY
YET MY BLINDNESS IS AS AFFLICTION
MY WEAKNESS REMAINS AS A SIN
MY STUMBLE IS THEIRS A SCOFF
MY FALL REMAINS THEIR DESIRE
YET WHO SHALL SAVE ME LORD
THE DERISIVE DARKNESS ENVELOPS
AS SUCH HANDS OF EVIL ABOUND
THEIR SPITTLE DRIPS FROM MY FACE
THEIR REVELRY REMAINS MY SORROW
THEIR HATRED REMAINS AS AN ASSAIL
THEIR ATTACKS REMAIN THE ASSAULT
THE LAUGHTER AS HIGH AS ETERNITY
CONDEMNATION DEEP AS AN ABYSS
YET REMAINING NO CLOAK OF COMFORT
AND NO CONSOLATIONS FOR WEEPING
AT THE DEEP GRAVES OF OUR PASSING
A SADNESS MOURNING OF OUR ELDERS
WHENCE ARE YOU HOLY LORD AND I
FROM THIS GHASTLY PLACE AN ASCENT

TOGETHER BOTH SHUNNED OF THE WORLD
BOTH CONDEMNED IN THE HEARTS OF MEN -
YET ONLY SUCH AN OBEDIENT DISCIPLINE
THE SAVING SURRENDER FROM ADAM'S SIN

DO WE HEAR SOUNDS OF EVERLASTING GLORY
DO WE SEE THE FLASHING OF THE YOURS ALONE THE PRESCRIBED
IN SALVATION
RISING ABOVE AMID THE ASHES THEIR SHEOL

TRUSTED TRUTH

O LORD,
DOES GOD PROVIDE A WARY WARE
DO MEN ABIDE HIS TRUSTED TRUTH

VIRTUE THINGS

O LORD,
WE PRAY HUMBLY TO GOD IN VIRTUE
THAT WE NEVER PRAY VAINLY THINGS

OBEDIENCE

O LORD,

IT IS THE FATHER'S RESPONSIBILITY TO PROVIDE ALL TRUTH
IT IS THE FATHER'S DUTY TO REVEAL AN ACTUAL TRUTH -
IT REMAINS A SON'S RESPONSIBILITY TO OBEY TRUTH -
IT IS THE SON'S DUTY TO RECEIVE OBEDIENCE TRUTH -

OBEY RECEIVE

THE INTELLECTUAL MEMORIAL WITHIN SPIRITUAL AS TRUTH

HOLY SOULS ADVANCE HOLY ACTION VIRTUE IN DUTY TRUTH

NATURAL SINFUL

O LORD,
THAT WE DENY OURSELVES WHAT IS SINFUL -
NEVER TO DENY THAT WHICH IS WHOLLY NATURAL
WITHIN YOUR SIGHT, THE SIGHT OF HOLY GOD, HIMSELF
THERE IS ONLY ONE DRUMMER WITH A MULTIPLE DRUMMING -
THERE REMAINS ONLY THE ONE FLUTIST IN SPIRITS OF MANY
TUNES -

COMMANDMENT LOVER

COMMANDMENTS ARE THE JUST GIFTS TO THE COMMANDER
OF LOVERS
A COMMANDED OF LOVERS WHOM BASK SUCH RUSHING ETERNAL
THE WIND

SANITY

O LORD,
SUCH SANITY THE MEN CLAIM THEMSELVES WHOLLY TRUTH
ARE WE INSANE TO UNDERSTANDING OUR OWN SINFULNESS

St Joseph Our Fathers

O LORD,
WHO WOULD BE WHOLLY AS ST JOSEPH
TO BE CALLED AS YOUR OWN FATHER
THAT YOU SHOULD TEACH HIM A
THING OR TWO, THAT A CHILD
IS FATHER TO THE MAN

ESSENCE

O LORD,
WE MAY PAINT THE MOON AND STARS WITH CREAM CHEESE,
YET THEY REMAIN ONLY AS THEY ARE YOUR OWN HOLY DUST -
AS MEN PERSIST TO MAKE OF THINGS WHAT THEY ARE NOT
STRIVING TO AVOID AN ESSENCE THAT OF WHICH THEY ARE -

AUTHENTICITY

O LORD,
TO BE THE WHOLLY AS HOLY IN GOD, AS WE ARE
TO AVOID THE PARTIALITY OF THE WORLDLY ILLUSION

SOMEWHAT AUDACIOUS AROUND

O LORD,
YOU WALK THE FACE OF THE EARTH TEACHING
TRUTH OF LOVE AND FORGIVENESS, NEVER ONCE
RENDERING THE BANE SCORECARD EVIDENCED.

-TEACHING TRUTH IS THE REVEALING PRESENCE
OF GOD, AND NEVER DIMINISHES INTO ANGRY
INSISTENCE THAT OTHERS DO OR BE AS YOU ARE.

-YOU EAT WITH SINNERS, YOU LIVE WITH SINNERS,
YOU TEACH WITH SINNERS, YET SOME SEEK A
HOLIEST THAN THOU ATTITUDE THAT SINNERS ARE LESS LOVED
IN VALUE, YET MORE JUDGED AS IN THE DISMISSAL DISSIPATION
FROM SALVATION.

SO, LORD, AM I HOLY - NO; AM I LOVED - YES.
IF NONE ELSE IS EVIDENT, IN TRUTH YOU TEACH.

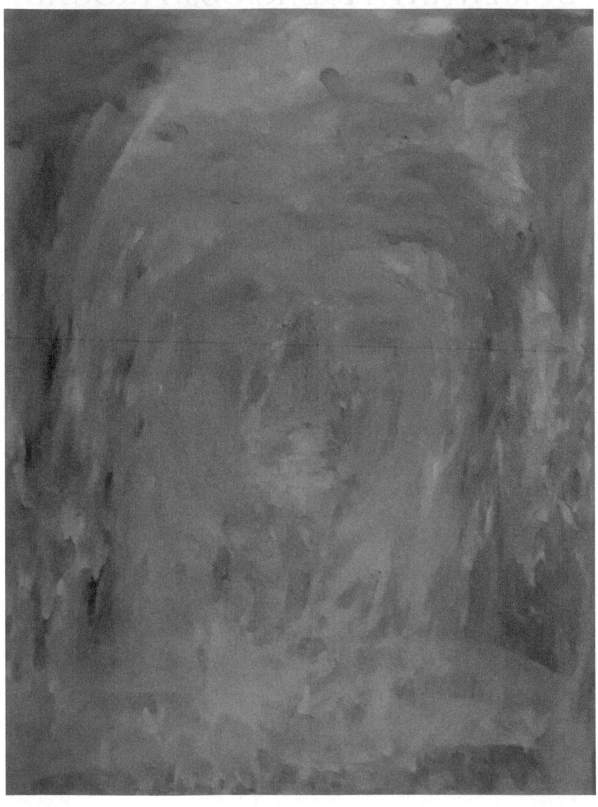

GO WITHIN MEDITATION

O LORD,
IF ONLY SUCH THAT WE NOT GET OF THE WORLD - SELFISH SELF
THOUGH INSTEAD GO WITHIN UNTO HOLY GOD - SOULFUL SELF
FOR WHAT REMAINS OF EARTH IS THAT OF SPIRIT SELF. UNTIL
RESURRECTION OF AN EARTHLY
AND THAT WHICH GOES TO GOD IS IN A WILL IN. SOUL. UNTO
RESURRECTION HEAVENLY
COMMENDABLE SPIRIT SELF IN HOLY HANDS SOUL WILL JUSTIFIES
RESURRECTION RESOLVE

FINAL JUDGEMENT DAY HIS. TERRIBLE DAY. LASTING INHERITANCE
JUSTICE AUSPICE

WEAKNESS OF MEN

HOLY MEN PRAY ALWAYS TO GOD IN FAITH
HUMBLE MEN CLEAN WORLDLY LATRINES
PROUD MEN GUARD VANITY THINGS
VAIN MEN SHOW PROWESS
REBELLIOUS MEN LACK HOLY TEMPERANCE
IGNORANT MEN LACK HOLY KNOWLEDGE
STUPID MEN LACK HOLY PRUDENCE
NAIVE MEN LACK HOLY FORTITUDE
DISAPPOINTED MEN LACK DISCIPLINED OBEDIENCE
DARKENED SPIRITS LACK AN OBEDIENCE DISCIPLINE

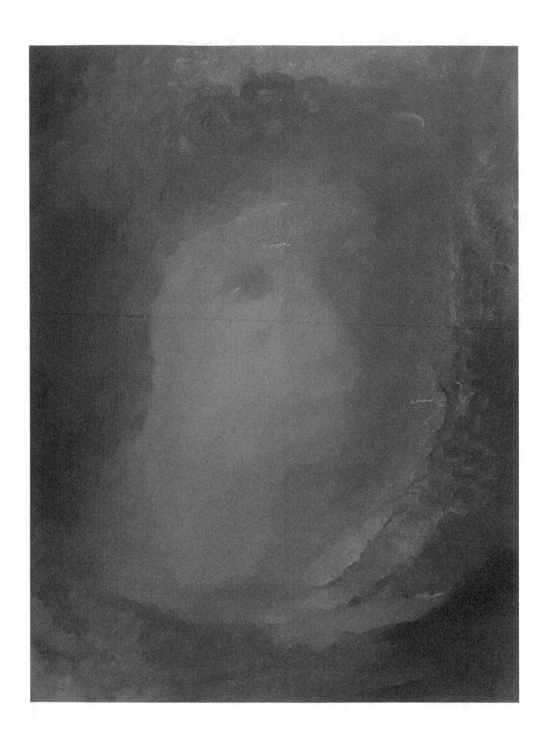

Persecution

ONE WHO PERSECUTES ANOTHER TO CONSIDER OF HIMSELF
AS TESTER AND TEACHER REVEALS TO WITHIN HIS OWN SELF
AN INADEQUACY AS EXPOSED A TEMPERED IRRELEVANCE.
FOR WHAT PURPOSE IS A LESSON THAN TEACHER LEARNING.
WHAT WILLS IN LESSON SERVES STUDENT TRANSFORMATION.
IN WHAT RESOLVE REMAINS GARNERED DIRECTIVE ASCENT.
TO WHOM ASCENDS SURRENDER OBEDIENCE DISCIPLINE.

O, LORD, MAY WE PERSEVERE WITHIN CHARITY GRATITUDE.

HIS NAME IS JESUS CHRIST

O LORD, THAT WE EVEN CONSIDER TO BREAK HOLY FETTERS
RIPPED INTO THE WRIT OF STONE ITSELF GARNERING TRUTH.
EVEN IF THE ENTIRE EARTH REBELS, YOU ARE WHOLLY HOLY
GOD, CREATOR AND DISSIPATION IN ALL, DESTINY THUS IN
REST DEEMS YOUR PURPOSE WILL RESOLVE FOREVER ASCENT.
THERE IS ONLY ONE LIFE, AND HIS NAME IS JESUS CHRIST,
WHO EACH OF MEN'S SOULS PONDERS A RESIDENCE WITHIN.

Appointment

MINDFULNESS IS DIALOG WITHIN COMMUNIQUE
HEART-FELT IS AS DISCOURSE WITHIN COURSING
SPIRITED-NESS IS DIRECTION WITH DIRECTIONAL

RESOLUTION IS DECISIVENESS WITHIN RESOLVE
STEADFASTNESS IS REST WITHIN THE STILLNESS. APPOINTMENT
IN ETERNAL

RESTLESSNESS IS MOVE WITHOUT A STILLNESS. DISAPPOINTMENT
TEMPORAL

O LORD, THAT WE MAY BE THUS REMAIN APPOINTED COURSING
DIRECTIONAL

THE HOLY BIBLE CONVERSION

GOD CHRIST — WATER IN SPIRIT OF WATER

NOAH ADAM — LIGHT IN WATER OF LIGHT

MOSES ELIJAH — FIRE IN LIGHT OF FIRE

PETER PAUL — LIFE IN FIRE OF LIFE

PRAYER

HOLY WAY PRAYER, FAVOR ASSIGNED BY YOU TO MEN,
EVEN AS SOME DANCE TO TUNES OF THOSE WHOM INTO
WORLDLY COMMAND DISREGARD AREAS OF PERFORMANCE
DUTIFULLY, HOLY AUSPICIOUS HUMILITY DIRE IN TOWARD
SUCCESSION APROPOS CONCOMITANT A FLAGRANCE, YET
SHALL WE MEEKLY IGNORE YOUR MOST SACRED TRUST IN
PURPOSE, AS DENIED BY SOME WHOM DO PERSIST TO
OVERSIGHTEDNESS

PRESUMPTION AN OWNED ARROGANCE AND HAUGHTINESS.

LORD, FORGIVE US OUR COMPLEXITY IN TOWARD IMPATIENCE
OF OTHERS, AS EVEN OUR OWN IMPATIENCE IMPERFECTION
CIRCUMSCRIBES SIMPLY WITHIN REVEALING AN UNKINDNESS
MUCH OUR OWN A BARTERED WITHOUT OUR INNER VISION

O Lord, A Freedom
from Their Sheol

LORD, DO DEMONS RELISH
THE SOULS AWAITING YOU,
THAT THEY TORTURE AS A
SHOWY CHEER FOR THEIR
CROWDS, ANCHORING NO

SOUND SUFFERING SELF,
YET ARROGANCE OF SOUL
TO TORTURE, TO DRAIN
EVERY OUNCE OF LIFE

IN MY OWN SOUL THAT
NO THING BE LEFT BUT
YOU, LIFE ITSELF, WHO
IS LIGHT IN THE WIND AND

FLAME IN MY OWN HEART,
THAT IT NEVER DESPAIRS A
WITHOUT YOU, YET ONLY AS

THE TORCH WITHIN SHINES
BRIGHTLY THE LIBERTY SELF
FROM THE SHEOL OF THEIR
DISPARAGEMENT AND THE

FREEDOM OF PERSON FROM
SWINDLERS IN SWINE THEIR
BOASTING WITHIN A CORPSE.

THE FROST LAMENT

O LORD,
YOU WASH MY HANDS CLEAN
SUFFERING AMID THE TEARS
OF MY OWN MOTHER WITHIN
ME EVEN AS MY OWN TEARS

UNITED WITH HERS AT THE
REVELRY OF OUR BROTHERS
RUNNING DASTARDLY DEEDS
AS THOUGH THE WINTER NEVER

COMES OR SPRING JUSTICE DOES

NO WARE TO LAST THE FROST OF THE
DAYS OWN DEW, YET SCREAMING
ABODES OF DAYS GONE BY AND THE
TOMORROWS OF YESTERYEAR GRACE
THE DUST AND CRY THE RIVERS STILL.

Sorrowful Disregard

O GOD
THEY CRUCIFY HIS NAKEDNESS
AS THOUGH IT IS REMISS THEIR
OWN SHAME YET ESPOUSED OF
A DECADENCE DEBAUCHERY IN

THE VEINS OF THEIR OWN LACK
OF PERPLEXITY THOUGH TEEMS

THEIR VEHEMENCE AND MOST

VAPID DISREGARD FOR THINGS
HOLY, BUT OF A RAMPANT EVIL.

THE GORGE OF FOREVER

WHERE TO GO WHAT TO DO
YET VALLEYS OF TEARS AND
MOUNTAINS FALLEN BEYOND
THE GRACE OF DAYS SO LONG

YET NEVER DERISIVE TOWARD
THE LACKING DISPLEASURE OF
A MAN GONE WRONG YET SUCH
WITHIN CONTRITION THE MIND

OF A WALLOW CASTS ITS SHADOW
TO THE WIND AND ITS RIVERS INTO

THE GORGE OF FOREVER THAT TIME
ITSELF HEALS THE RIFTS AS BEYOND

ETERNAL INFINITUDE IN A GRANDEUR
ADVANCE EXCELLENCE TO THE GLORY
OF GOD AND ANGELS FOR THE SAINTS.

PITY NOT MY SOUL

PITY NOT MY OWN SOUL
O LORD, THAT I MAY SEE
WITHIN THE COMPANY
SO WELL THINE OWN KEEP

TO FOSTER THE GRAIN OF
SUSTENANCE AND WINE
OF YOUR HOLY TO BRING
TO BEAR ITS FRUIT DUE IN

SEASONS OF TIME FORECAST
WELL GRAZED THE PENDULUM
OF TIME AS WIND MERE ETERNAL

An Eternal Ire

O LORD
HEARTS ARE REMEMBERED AMID
THE BROKENNESS LOSS AT TIMES OF
A HOPE ETERNAL, YET TOMORROWS
OF WHOLE FAITH IN LOVE WITH HOPE

DO PAINT THE CASCADE ITS STREAMING
THE LOVELIER GRANDEUR OF ETERNAL IRE.

AWE SO EMINENT

O LORD,
IS IT MY NEUROSIS TO GRATIFY
THE SEMBLANCE OF TIME PASSING
NE'ER THE NOTICE OF ETERNAL PRESENCE

BEING MY OWN LACK OF INTERIOR VISION
THE BEATIFIC ANGELIC ITS AWE SO EMINENT

THE PROMISE

O LORD,

EVER WE LOOK O THINGS PASSING
YET FORGET WE NEVER THE PROMISE
ETERNAL IN PRESENCE STANDING TRUTH

ITS OWN COVENANT FOR THE WHOLENESS OF
ITS BIRTH SO PREDOMINANT EVIDENT PREVALENT

OCEANS OF TEARS

EVIL WIND I SAY THIS WORLD TO BE
FOR I AM BUT THE SINNER FORLORN
WASTED AWAY AMONG THORNS OF
ROSES LONG FORGOTTEN AS MEN THEIR

KNEES PRETEND THEIR HUMBLE EYES OF
GLASS TO REFLECT NO PRISM. DARE WE
SAY LORD THAT EVER IS THE MOST WRETCHED
OF MEN BARE WITHIN MY SOUL A HARP TO PRAISE

THEE AS ANGELS TO SING THINE ARIAS OF FOREVER
MORE AND TIDINGS ETERNAL LEST THEY GREET A
DAWN BEFORE ITS SETTING SUN AND THE ROOF OF
THE SKY BEFORE ALL THE VILER MAN CONFESSES. NEED
BE LORD BEFORE US RESTS OUR EQUITY LEVELING FOR NO MORE
TO WEEP ONLY SORROW THE BARE FOR THEY AS
I DID STUMBLE TO FALL TOWARD ETERNAL MISGIVINGS
OF TRUE LIFE AND ITS NAME FOR THE CALL.

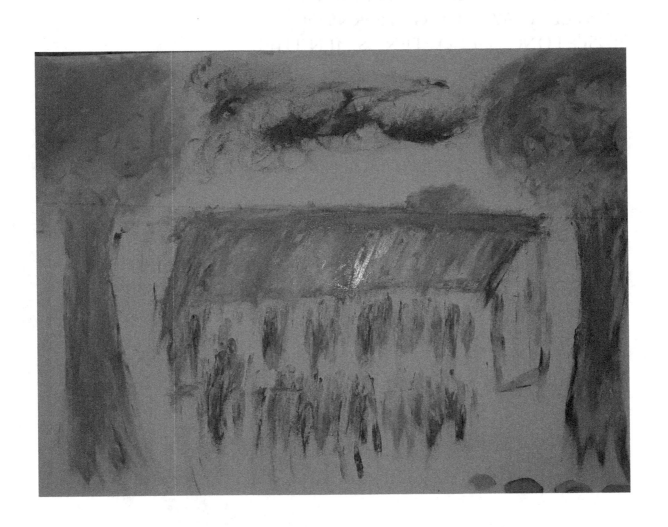

IN HIS NAME THRU FATHER
WITH SON IN HOLY SPIRIT
AMEN AMEN AMEN AMEN

KUDOS KUMBAYA

Printed in the United States
By Bookmasters